FLYOVER COUNTRY

PRINCETON SERIES OF CONTEMPORARY POETS

Susan Stewart, series editor

For other titles in the Princeton Series of Contemporary Poets see page 115

FLYOVER COUNTRY

Poems

Austin Smith

PRINCETON UNIVERSITY PRESS
Princeton and Oxford

Published by Princeton University Press
41 William Street, Princeton, New Jersey 08540
6 Oxford Street, Woodstock, Oxfordshire OX20 1TR

press.princeton.edu

Library of Congress Control Number: 2018930998

ISBN: 978-0-691-18156-1

ISBN (pbk.) 978-0-691-18157-8

British Library Cataloging-in-Publication Data is available

Acquisitions Editor: Anne Savarese
Editorial Assistant: Thalia Leaf
Production Editorial: Ellen Foos
Text and cover design: Pamela Schnitter
Cover image: Aerial view above pivot irrigation circles,
Edward County, Kansas. Aerial Archives / Alamy Stock Photo
Production: Jacqueline Poirier
Copyeditor: Jodi Beder

This book has been composed in Adobe Garamond Pro and ScalaSans OT

Printed on acid-free paper. ∞

Printed in the United States of America

10 9 8 7 6 5 4 3 2 1

FOR HOLLY MULDER-WOLLAN

Contents

To Go to Lena   1

I

Into the Corn   7
Fences   9
The Raccoon Tree   11
Cat Moving Kittens   12
Beyond Mirror Lake   13
The Windbreak   15
American Glue Factory   17
Chekhov   18
Three Radios   20
Hired Hands   22
Water Witching   24
Apparition of Knives   26
Scrapper Kevin   27
The Vampire   29
Building a Temple for the Field Mice   30
Father and Son: Barcelona   32
Grasshoppers   33
Some Haiku Found Scrawled in the Margins of *The Old Farmer's Almanac 1957*   34

II

The Mechanic's Children   39
The Shaker Abecedarius   40
The Streets of Turin   41
Outside the Anne Frank House   43
The Crutches at Lourdes   45
The Only Tavern in Hyde, Wisconsin   46
The Spider   48
Factory Town   49
Street Performer: Asheville, North Carolina   51

The Bow   52

Cottonpicker   54

Atomic Fireball   55

Soap Operas   56

The Blind   57

The Bombing of Hospitals   58

Wounded Men Seldom Come Home to Die   60

Elegy for Thomas Merton   62

Premature Elegy for Claude Eatherly   65

We Defy Augury   66

The Man without Oxen Trembles   67

Swatting Flies   69

That Particular Village   71

Drone   74

The Witness Tree   76

III

Cicadas   81

Flyover Country   83

Dark Day   85

White Lie   87

The Capacity of Speech   88

N Judah   89

Break in the Weather   90

Dead Dogs   92

Growing Cold   94

Lament of the Man Who Picks Up Dead Animals   96

Country Things   97

Ode to Flour   99

Things We Don't Often Think Of   101

Film of the Building of a Coffin Viewed in Reverse   103

The Twain   105

Feathers   107

The Light at the End   108

Notes   111

Acknowledgments   113

Heart of the prairie
My heart
The world still finds it and I
Still fall apart
Prairie chase away the weariness
Prairie chase away all of it

Ghost in the canyon
If I can open my eyes
This feather and my life will
Fly, fly

—JASON MOLINA, "Heart My Heart"

FLYOVER COUNTRY

TO GO TO LENA

To go to Lena, you must leave
The highway and take
The way of wheat. You must go
Across country, follow deer
Paths and cattle trails, climb
Over barbwire fences, cross
Nameless creeks swollen
With ag runoff and rain and sleep
Wherever the dark finds you.
At dawn, when redwing blackbirds
Accost you, show them the visa of blood
You were issued in the brambles
And they'll permit you to pass,
But don't bother asking them
The way to Lena. Better to save
Your breath for the journey.
Know that anything claiming
To know the way to Lena is lying.
Don't trust the bullet-riddled signs.
The map you carry is obsolete.
Better to burn it. See no one
Wants you to visit Lena, the town
Of Lena least of all. All it wants
Is to die in peace. But walk
Far enough and you can't help
But reach Lena one day.
Approaching porches, you'll find
Rocking chairs still rocking,

Swings swaying, geraniums
In clay pots, but no one
Will answer your knocking.
In the park the carousel is spinning,
The painted horses galloping,
Impaled by bright brass rods,
But there's no one selling tickets.
Downtown, where Main Street
Stretches out like an arm gone
White from the tourniquet,
The theater plays the same film
Over and over. You sit in the back
Row and watch the matinee.
You should know that if you
Go to Lena you may
Never leave. You may
Find yourself one day
Behind the counter of the pawn shop,
Appraising freshwater pearls, or holding
A pair of scissors, having become
The town's only barber. Come
Evening, you don't know whose
Hair it is you're sweeping up.
Now, deep in the stacks
Of the library, shelving a novel
Thirty years overdue,
You thumb through it, remembering
The day you checked it out.
Tending bar that night for no one,
You don't even bother
Swatting the flies that crawl
Through your arm hair,
Feeling an intimacy
You haven't felt in years.
You've forgotten exactly

When it was you came to Lena,
What time of year, spring or fall,
Nor can you remember why.
One morning, working at the post office,
A letter comes bearing your name.
You slip it into your mail pouch
And deliver it to yourself.
When you get home that evening,
You open it. A young man
Has written you, wanting to know
How to get to Lena. You sit
In the porch swing at twilight,
Considering how to
Answer him. Finally, you go
Up to your room and by
The last light begin to write:
To go to Lena, you must leave
The highway and take
The way of wheat . . .

I

INTO THE CORN

In summer we were warned not to enter it
If the tassels were head-high or higher
Lest we get lost like the boy who went in
After a ball called foul and never came out

Whose parents must have been decades dead
But who himself had not aged a day
Who runs bases wherever farm boys say
Ghost man oh ghost man we need you!

Out of longing to enter it we reached in
The leaves slicing our arms like the knife
My mother used to slash the risen dough
Wrenching the ears off the stalks

Like twisting doorknobs in the dark
We held them to our own ears grinning
Before turning serious and regretful
For through them we had heard the boy laughing

And as we brusquely shucked the husks
Like village grandmothers sitting in doorways
Down to the slick light green inner leaves
We longed for the moist dark that seemed to us

One of the privileges of being born as corn
But not knowing this longing was common

We held the silk under our armpits instead
And laughed at the long joke of adolescence

We were soon to be the punchlines of
While privately recalling the pubic hair
Of women we'd seen in porn magazines
Found in a bag of trash at the farm's edge

When the tender kernels were exposed
In their wavering rows we gnawed them
Like they were sweet corn picked
Up at the roadside stand for supper

Boiled in sugar-water buttered and salted
To be spun on the lathes of our hands
And when we'd bitten off more than
We could chew we snapped

The cobs clean in half
So as to see the pith and believe
We'd gone at least as far into the corn
As that boy who'd disappeared had

FENCES

Some to separate
Pasture from pasture in order
To clarify the prairie,

Others to surround the farm,
Keeping the world
Out and the herd in.

Between the barbs designed
To bloom at intervals
Measuring the span of a hand,

Redwing blackbirds scolded
Both nations of grass
The fence divided.

The posts that stood
Where they'd been driven
Knee-deep in limestone

Had begun to lean
Like men forced to march
Into the wind.

And where oak saplings
Had had the audacity to grow,
They'd had no choice

But to swallow the wire,
Remembering via rings
The anniversary of that first summer

They sensed the wire tapping
Their bodies, then began,
Tentatively, to accept it,

To take it in, feeling
The wire grow taut
In the grip of their bark,

Until they began to believe
They needed it
In order to stand.

THE RACCOON TREE

Winter to winter
We could never quite remember
Where in the woods it was,
And so would have to find it again,
Part of me doubting it
Had ever existed.
But then there it would be,
The oak with the dark
Slit in its side, darker if
The ground around it
Was aglow with snow.
Elbowing one another to peer in,
We thought the tree empty
Until our eyes adjusted.
Then would appear
The pair of green eyes,
Then the telltale mask
And ringed tail, this creature
Who every winter
Hid in fear of us
Boys who came without fail
To fill its world
With breath and darkness.

CAT MOVING KITTENS

We must have known,
Even as we reached
Down to touch them
Where we'd found them

Shut-eyed and trembling
Under a straw bale
In the haymow, that
She would move them

That night under cover
Of darkness, and that
By finding them
We were making certain

We wouldn't see them again
Until we saw them
Crouching under the pickup
Like sullen teens, having gone

As wild by then as they'd gone
Still in her mouth that night
She made a decision
Any mother might make

Upon guessing the intentions
Of the state: to go and to
Go now, taking everything
You love between your teeth.

BEYOND MIRROR LAKE

Left the city before the first sirens.
Crossed the bridge, crossed the valley,
Its blossoming orchards and dormant crosses.
Let the car carry me against the streams
Running the other way, as if they knew something
I didn't. Reached Yosemite. Paid my fee. Left keys,
Wallet, phone, everything identifying me behind
And started up the path to Mirror Lake.
Passed tourists taking selfies, backpackers consulting maps.
Beyond the lake: no one. The trail narrowing, the light
Floating up the sheer cliffs, leaving the valley
In shadow. A branch held a blue flannel shirt
Out for me. It gave me a chill, being offered clothes
Clear out there, but it was nothing compared
To the chill a dead oak gave me like a ring
Last worn by the dead. I stopped
As if ordered to, having never seen a tree
Tremble like that tree was trembling, the tambourines
Of its dry leaves rattling in a breeze that didn't stir
Those of any other tree. The thing that spooked me
About the leaves was how perfect they were even though
They were dead, like the willow motif carved
Into the headboard of my childhood bed.
It was as if they were trying to pass for living leaves
And in so doing betrayed the tree, like stars
Sewn onto clothing. The tree seemed to be shivering
And I felt I had come to the place where
The earth fears for herself. This fear was nothing

Like our fear of terror or the warming of the planet
But a wordless, private fear we were never
Meant to know. And I felt like a boy who,
Hearing a strange sound upstairs, climbs
The steps and sees, through the keyhole,
His father weeping, and knows that
What has always been so
Certain will never be certain again.

THE WINDBREAK

The morning after the evening
He came home early to tell us
The radiologist had seen something
In the X-rays of his lungs
I decided to clear the tangle
Of nightshade and thorns
That grew under the pines
Like I was erasing scribble
The brush fought back at first
Threw birds at my eyes
Rolled rabbits at my legs
But I angled the chainsaw in severing
The whole mess at the root
And dragged it out like people
In hiding betrayed by a cough
I wanted all that growth gone
So we could see clear through
The windbreak to Winneshiek Road
The pile of limbs grew and within
A week the blue-pink pines
Sprang clean out of the brown
Needle-strewn ground
But while waiting for a day
The wind was right to light
The pile on fire I began regretting
What I'd done the mass eviction
I'd served innocent creatures
In the dead of winter

The rabbits seeking refuge
In the asylum of the snow
The birds flown to other farms
Nothing stood between us now
And the plow-scoured road
Down which he came the evening
I set the pile on fire
To tell us that
The young radiologist had made a mistake
It was nothing
A blemish on the X-ray
And I spent the whole next day
Shoveling ashes

AMERICAN GLUE FACTORY

for Rachel Carson

All your childhood you watched
Old horses file up a wooden ramp
Into the American Glue Factory
And file out as smoke.
This was in Springdale, Pennsylvania,
Up the Allegheny from Pittsburgh,
In the early part of the twentieth century.
Though it was never mentioned, you knew
What the horses were being turned into.
In your desk at school was a bottle
You used to join this and that
To this and that. You knew horses
Were what hung the gold and silver
Stars in the firmament of your notebook,
What made the hearts stick
In the valentine you never gave
That girl at school. Summer nights
The stench of burning
Horses drove you into the house
From the screen porch where you sat
Reading about the sea.
It was there you first learned that
Something in the air can close a story.

CHEKHOV

They say you may have caught
Tuberculosis from the peasants
Who came to Melikhovo

To be seen by you. Hearing them
Coughing in the hall, you put down
Your pen and rose from your desk.

Short of breath, they had traveled
All night to arrive by dawn, drawn
By rumors of your kindness.

While you warmed the stethoscope
In your hands and the old farmer
Bared his chest, your character

Stood patiently on the doorstep,
Holding a letter of introduction
You had yet to write. The longer

You spent away from the story
The harder it would be to finish it,
But the hall was long, the line

Out the door, and you would turn
None away, knowing how far
They had come for the comfort

Of having someone
Listen to their lungs and say it
Sounded better than it sounded

While you stood breathing
In their sighs of relief,
Saying, softly, "Next."

THREE RADIOS

December 7th, 1941

It balanced on a beam above
My grandfather where he sat
Milking sixteen Holsteins
By hand in stanchions.

When he heard the words
Pearl Harbor over the jets
Of milk ringing in the pail,
Their markings seemed to him
White archipelagos
In black water.

November 22nd, 1963

It stood in the living room,
As significant a presence
As any piece of furniture,
A piece of furniture that talked
To my grandmother of the world
While she polished wood.

When, at one in the afternoon,
It pronounced the president dead,
She shushed it
And anointed it with lemon oil.

September 11th, 2001

Manure-spattered, it sat
On a shelf along the wall
Of the pit parlor.

Over the churning
Of the milking machines
My father heard the anchor
Cry out when the second plane
Struck the other tower.

Only then did he turn
The radio up, the antenna
Trained violently toward town.

HIRED HANDS

Hired hands of my grandfather's
Time haunt me. They come floating
Through the doorframes of meth
Houses on the verge of exploding,
Touching at the pale wrists
Just above where they've been snipped
Like two hyacinths. They follow me
Into the barn I've slipped into
To look for something, I've forgotten
What. Their ring fingers are
Ringless but the hands are married
To one another. They make
For my hair, tousle it, then fly
Up into the rafters like two doves
Or one owl. From down here
I can just make out the harvest
Moons of the bones. Somewhere
In the poisoned dirt of this county
A man my grandfather hired
In 1957 out of pity for his wife
And kids waiting anxiously in the car
Lies handless in his coffin,
Having not yet awoken to the fact
His hands are in the habit of leaving him.
Oh but who can blame them
For wanting to go out
Pickpocketing? They take
Nothing valuable. And I for one

Understand their need to feel
Up the thin summer dresses
Billowing under the church pews.
The young women know
It is only the breath of God.
When they've had their fun,
The hands let themselves back in
To the cheap motel room
Of the grave, opening the door
Quietly so as not to wake him.
For if he were to learn that
His hands have been leaving him,
He would find a way to follow
Them into the world
And make some real trouble.

WATER WITCHING

A pipe burst in the night.
Our father dug all morning.
At noon he climbed out
Of the earth and went in
To call the man who finds water.

He came out in the evening,
A wizard with his beard
And forked wand of willow.
A bachelor, he had never
Found a wife, spent his life

In search of water. Our father
Told us to watch him
As if we might learn something,
Or as if he was not to be trusted,
And went off to bring the cows in.

We watched him walk slowly
Back and forth, the wand
So light in his hand it seemed
To flinch with some invisible power.
Sometimes he stopped as if listening.

Finally, as if admitting failure,
He beckoned us, asked
Did we have anything

In our pockets? I offered him
An old pocketknife seized

With rust. He opened
The reluctant blade and, kneeling,
Stabbed it into the grass to mark where
We should dig. And when I tried
To close the knife, I couldn't.

APPARITION OF KNIVES

Stuck in the side of a barn outside Lanark
Are eighteen knives in the shape of a woman.
Rust streaks on the wall make it seem
As if she is veiled and perpetually rising.
The blades are plunged so deep in the boards
The points stick through the other side
And glitter in the dark like stars.
The wood handles are long enough for pigeons
To perch on. If you approach this apparition
Of knives, they will take wing in a flock
That roughly approximates her. No one knows
Who threw the knives, or who volunteered
To stand against the wall to give the one
Who threw them a body to trace. The only ones
Who visit the apparition are teenage lovers
Who take turns taking pictures of each other
Framed in knives and a priest who believes that
No human hand threw them, that the knives
Slipped out of the drawers of farmhouse kitchens
And hovered over the pasture in formation
Like fighter jets before plunging together
Into the wall. It is said that if you pull a knife
Out you will bleed to death the next time
You cut yourself. It is said also that once
Upon a time there were nineteen knives.

SCRAPPER KEVIN

They call me Scrapper Kevin,
You know why?
It's how I make a living.
Scrap metal.
Can't fault a guy for making a living
Any way a guy can.
But people around here,
A lot of 'em hate me.
That guy there, for instance.
Jesus Christ
Don't look at him.
That guy's here to kill me.
There's a hit out on me see.
See there's this pond in the woods
Back there, you don't know it,
Don't nobody know it
Until they go in there.
People miss the curve
And go right clear
Through the brush.
There's gotta be ten,
A dozen cars in there,
Some with bodies in 'em,
Bodies still in 'em.
Everybody knows that.
You don't gotta be a genius.
This guy who put the hit out on me,
His daughter drowned in there.

She was texting him.
He's the one started the rumor
I've been dragging cars up out of there,
Selling 'em for cash.
He hired that guy there
To kill me. That's why
I'm talking to you
So's not to give him the chance.
Their plan's to throw me in there,
See how I like it.
Don't think I don't know.
This here's a small town,
La Honda's a small town.
I swear to God, I don't care
How broke I get,
I'll never go in there.
Can you imagine?
Those bodies in there,
Years some of them
Bodies been in there.
I know what they must look like.
I'm from Michigan.
Every winter some kids'd get drunk
And drive out on the ice,
Thinking it was thick enough
To hold 'em.
I wouldn't go in that water
To save my life
But I'm not gonna lie.
Sometimes driving by I think
Man all that metal.

THE VAMPIRE

The poor man probably just worked third-shift
at Honeywell where they made light switches
before the outsourcing, but we convinced ourselves that
Behind the drawn yellow curtains the color
of mustard and the signs in the yard admonishing us
to keep out lived a vampire. Across the street
sprawled Lincoln Cemetery, and *maybe this is why*
I imagined that like Lincoln the vampire was tall
and gaunt, lying long in a coffin he had built himself.
How deep must the sleep of small-town vampires be
so similar to the sleep of weary fathers, or of men
who've lost sons, who sleep in the light of the muted
world news, for whom our dusk is dawn and our
dawn dusk, who *it isn't true* drink one vial of blood
every evening as some swear by one glass of red
wine to conclude the rude workday with a little grace,
who *don't* visit the new graves in fresh thirst,
who are *not* evil and *don't* deserve to die gasping
around the silver letter opener of a hero. I'm *not*
glad we threw the rock through his window and ran.
I'm *not* glad we woke the vampire. I *don't* hope
the sudden inrush of light killed him. Trust me,
the sick motherfucker *probably a father holding*
his son's purple heart or a very tired man crying
in his bed littered with glass deserved to die.

BUILDING A TEMPLE FOR
THE FIELD MICE

The man who spent his life
In iron is retiring this year.

Most nights he leaves the house
And follows his shadow out

Like one man following another
Out of the bar to settle it, his hands

Shaking with the loaded dice of age.
In the middle of the pasture stands

A temple assembled from the skeletons
Of field mice. The man took something

Someone said to him once
To heart and now, years later,

There is only one last bone to place,
But it belongs in the innermost sanctum

And his hands are too big and tremble
Too much to fit inside. He knows that

The temple will never be finished
But, kneeling here night after night,

He has learned what it means
To pray.

FATHER AND SON: BARCELONA

One day many years from now
After your father has failed

To remember your name
You will only faintly remember

This night he carried you home
Through the streets of the Gothic Quarter

Your ash-colored lashes closing
And fluttering open

Closing and fluttering open
And the faint scent of lather on his neck

Unfair that I a stranger
Will remember him carrying you

While he will die and not remember
And you will live only faintly remembering

But to be alive is to be carried
By your father through your city

And laid in your bed without waking
Then opening your eyes in the morning

GRASSHOPPERS

Midsummer, I remember them
Bolting against my bare legs,
A green, sexual strength.
August found them strewn
In the dust like busted springs.
I touched them with my shoe
To make sure
They were dead
Before picking them up.
Packed tight on my dresser,
The jars looked like
Those homemade bombs
Filled with nails
No one
But the terrorist knows
Never went off.

SOME HAIKU FOUND SCRAWLED IN THE MARGINS OF *THE OLD FARMER'S ALMANAC 1957*

In the garden
All morning, tending,
Being tended.

―――

Alone with his father,
The boy fishes
With a bare hook.

―――

Summer dusk—
Lovers flirting
On the propane tank.

―――

One cork pushed in
Deeper than the other—
Summer night.

―――

Winter orchard—
Hard to say
Which are dying.

―――

No one owns
A favorite
Skipping stone.

———

In the window
The farmwife moves
To a different pane.

———

Museum in winter—
In the dinosaur skeleton,
A few bones missing.

———

Late-night diner—
A lot of silverware
For one mouth.

———

Barely restraining themselves
While we entertain guests—
The mousetraps.

———

Too small to hold any face—
The mirror
In her dollhouse.

———

Bankrupt tavern—
All the darts
Crammed in the bull's-eye.

———

Late winter—
The ventriloquist
Loses his voice.

———

Drafty farmhouse—
All the wicks
Curved the same way.

———

So light they might
Rise from my hand—
Baby teeth.

———

Practicing
Kissing the boy
Makes the mirror blush.

———

Call from the hospital—
The tea water
Boils itself away.

———

Toy soldier—
Something off
About his face.

II

THE MECHANIC'S CHILDREN

Barefoot in a spring,
Their feet white and cold as turnips,
Her dress pulled up, his pants
Rolled past his knees.
Each holds a jelly jar.

Imagine a tiny pair of glass lungs
Hovering in the green woods,
Inhaling murky water that was crystal
Clear this morning when they lay
Sleeping in the bed they share.

They're after the creatures that toil
In the sand, tireless as pacemakers.
The cracked crankcases of the cars
Their father abandoned
Bleed rainbows of oil.

When they see color in the water
They catch it too.
And long after all
The creatures they've caught have died
The rainbows will abide.

THE SHAKER ABECEDARIUS

Aunt Harriet, who raised my grandfather after his mother died,
Bought me a book before I was born called *The Shaker Abecedarius*. The
Cover showed traditionally antagonistic creatures getting along: a
Docile bull beside a lion with a lamb lying in his lap, a cat and a rabbit,
Each turned away from the other, under a table laden with
Fruit. I never met Aunt Harriet, who died before I could read, nor could I
Grasp what I was looking at as my mother turned the pages in that farm-
House out in the country. When I was old enough to understand
It, the book scared me. I knew it had been given me by a woman who was
    dying
Just as I was being born, and so I always associated the book with death, and
Kept it hidden beneath other books, big picture books of dinosaurs and
    the sea,
Looking at *The Shaker Abecedarius* only when a sorrow rose in
Me that could only be vanquished by fear. This is how I found myself some
Nights kneeling on the floor of my bedroom, to which I had been exiled,
Opening the book to find my name in the inside cover, scrawled in fading
Pencil, in Aunt Harriet's hand. She'd known my name before I did. So
Quickly did I turn the pages, anxious to reach the end, that I hardly
Read the names of the animals, which were strange, as if the
Shakers had known species that had long ago vanished from the face of
The Earth. I don't know why I was so afraid of that book. Maybe I didn't
Understand yet that the dead want nothing to do with us, that the Bible
Verses weren't being whispered to me by Aunt Harriet, but were being
Whispered to Aunt Harriet by me. Only when I turned the page to see
Xantus's hummingbird did I know I was nearing the end, the way
You know you are coming to the last cage in the city
Zoo when the sorrow of seeing so many animals starts to dawn on you.

THE STREETS OF TURIN

On the 3rd of January in the year 1889
While walking the streets of Turin
The philosopher Nietzsche saw a man
Flogging a horse in the one of the piazzas of Turin
The horse was refusing to pull a carriage in which
Sat a couple late for the theater in Turin
The horse had just come from the country
And was spooked by the commotion of Turin
Because it wore blinders and could not see
All the horse knew of the city of Turin
Were the cries of vendors and the whistles of police
And the cobblestone streets of Turin
That blurred between its hooves as its master urged
It to trot faster through the streets of Turin
The philosopher Nietzsche saw this horse being flogged
By a productive citizen of Turin
The reins having become whips in the hands of this man
Who made his living on the streets of Turin
But no one else so much as stopped or stared
As they crossed the Piazza Carlo Alberto in Turin
Shopping for food they would prepare that evening
When the shadows lengthened across Turin
And the lamps were lit in the quiet kitchens
Of the homes of the good people of Turin
So the man who'd declared that God was dead
Pushed his way through the crowds of Turin
Throwing his body between the man and the horse
Being whipped on the streets of Turin

Throwing his arms around the horse's strong neck
As if to save all of Turin
So that the lashes licked his hands like flames
And he fell sobbing onto the streets of Turin
Crying out for the poor horse to be spared
Being whipped by this man in Turin
Two policemen ran up blowing whistles in order
To see what was disturbing the peace of Turin
And as the driver apologized to the couple
Waiting patiently to be driven through Turin
The policemen carried the weeping philosopher away
And put him in a hospital in Turin
Where he wrote long rambling letters to strangers
Who had never set foot in Turin
One ordering the German emperor to go to Rome to be shot
All from the quiet of his room in Turin
While through the open window came the clop-clop-clop
Of the hooves of the horses of Turin
Including the horse he'd tried to save
Accustomed now to the commotion of Turin
As for the philosopher they put him in a mental institution
And he died a decade later in a villa in Weimar

OUTSIDE THE ANNE FRANK HOUSE

We bend knees, shift
Weight from foot
To foot, talk to those
We came with.
A few grow impatient
And leave. The line
Lurches forward.
Somewhere in the museum
They've built to house it
Stands the house itself.
I love every brick
In the walls, the very clay
They were shaped from.
The house is still
Doing what it has always done:
Taking people in.
A cold wind blows
Down the Prinsengracht.
We unzip bags, pull coats
Out by the sleeve.
The couple ahead
Of me leave. I watch them
Turn to one another
And agree.
It isn't worth the wait,
Their eyes seem to say.
They'll find a café.

I stay. I shuffle forward
With the others, thinking
Of all the lines we form
On Earth and what for.

THE CRUTCHES AT LOURDES

They came here two by two, carrying their cripple
Between them, saying to one another in snide whispers

Before and behind the foot, "Where does he think he's going?"
Or, "How quickly she moves today, as if she didn't need us!"

Left standing by the thousand now in the cool of the grotto,
They remember how ungratefully they were heaved here,

How thankless the miraculously cured were towards they
Who carried them miles and years and never once complained

About being stuffed in an armpit all their lives. The canes
Are even more morose than the crutches: they have no companion

To keep them company when night falls and the healed have gone
Off under their own power. The only way these crutches stand

A chance to walk again is if a pilgrim who comes here
Not only is not healed, but also suffers more and more

The lower he lowers himself into the waters his daughters
Claimed would cure him; so that he goes from merely crippled

To totally lame, and, to go home, has to take up a pair
Of crutches and leave behind his favorite swan-head cane.

THE ONLY TAVERN IN HYDE,
WISCONSIN

When I walked into the forest
Of camouflage, faces turned,
Gleaming through the leaves
Like tin plates hung
Amongst trees for targets.

In a moment of silence,
The eyes darted birdlike
Measuring what had wandered in.

Then the forest broke apart
Into forms, voices, hands
Emerged holding bottles,
Bodies lumbered toward the bar,
Wreathed by smoke
Like a forest restless with fire.

And the tree-sized men
Turned back to their game
Of euchre, torsos thick as trunks,
Arms the breadth of branches,
Fingers splayed twig-like
Holding their cards like leaves,
Which they turned as if acting
Out autumn.

And then I noticed
On every wall
The heads of deer,
Their glass eyes staring
Through years of dust
At the men who had killed them.

THE SPIDER

It is loneliness that makes me
Tie little bows of silk to leaf,
Branch, blade and blossom.
I build my web for the company,
Not the blood. O I love
The blood, of course: a vintage
In which you taste a year
Your ancestors knew.
But it isn't blood
That sustains me: it is
The shiver through the web
Like a doorbell tripping
Up the stairs of an empty manse.
I hurry over as if to help them,
But before they can beg me
For mercy I am turning them
Like a spindle on a lathe,
Their cries growing
Softer with each orbit,
Until I can hardly
Hear them hum.
Then I am lonely again,
A poet between poems.

FACTORY TOWN

The factory stands on the train
Of your town's wedding gown,
Dirtying it and smoking

Unfiltered cigarettes. Embarrassed,
The clouds rush to cover up
The track marks of the stars.

On your way home from the theater
The factory runs, it's too dark to say
Hello to the pale-faced people

Plummeting past you and your son.
Who knows what bright things
They conceal in their black coats

Now that they've rationed the rations.
Home before curfew, the iodine
Tablets fume in the bedtime

Glass of water your son requests.
He sips it as if it were hot tea
While you read to him yet again

That ancient story you three
Loved. You stumble over the new
Language but even it is becoming

Familiar. You close the book,
Kiss his forehead, stand the flashlight
Upright by the fuming glass

And stumble to your bed in the dark.
Your son will wake in the night
And turn on the flashlight

So he can see the water
That he will turn into urine
That you will carry in an armful

Of sheets down to the river,
That gray, dappled,
Broken thing running

Through the sickly trees
Like an app
-aloosa spooked by gunfire.

STREET PERFORMER: ASHEVILLE, NORTH CAROLINA

She stands completely still and completely
Silver: in her silver hands she holds silver
Drumsticks: the space between their tips
And the silver skin of her drum betrays her
Heartbeat, otherwise I might believe that
She was a statue. On a silver box draped
In silver cloth, her feet are bare and silver.
Silver her ears, silver her lips, silver her
Hair. Her dress is silver, the pleats
Like long knives: if, careless, I were
To brush my arm against one I am sure
I would bleed. I throw three quarters
Into her silver pail and her silver eyelids
Tremble open heavily like the wings
Of a housefly who's flown into paint.
By now I've slipped back into the crowd
But her eyes accuse me of being the one
Who woke her. They're the brown of rivers
After spring rains, the sole silverless thing
About her. I feel the way I felt when I
Was a child and my persistent curiosity
Overthrew every bastion of mystery.
She plays taps, a staccato battle-rattle,
But the weight of all that silver exhausts her.
Her head nods, her eyelids close,
And a boy asks his father for a quarter.

THE BOW

Every June we boys were given a gift
To share, to live the long summer through with
Because we lived far from everywhere
And any toy, no matter how small, could still
Fill the empty hours. One summer the gift
Was a bow and its flock of lithe arrows.
Even before we saw the boy on the box
We knew what a bow looked like when drawn
From the paintings of Frederic Remington.
But because he was our father it fell to him
To demonstrate how to shoot an arrow straight,
Though I doubt now he had ever shot
An arrow before. We winced as the ends
Neared one another as if the point was
To restore the bow to the full circle
It had been. It broke. I'll never
Be able to unremember how the slivers
Of fiberglass rayed through his poor palm
Like the quills of pheasant feathers we found
In the pasture and that he kept a bouquet of
On his desk. Had he tried to close his hand
Into a fist in anger at the pain, he couldn't have.
Our only consolation was knowing that
His strength had shattered it, not any weakness
In the bow. When he ran in to run hot water
Over his hand to coax the slivers out,
I plucked the arrow from where it had sprung

Sapling-like out of the grass
Ten feet from where the oak stood,
Having hoped for his sake
He would sink it into heartwood.

COTTONPICKER

I heard it all my childhood, this curse
My father and grandfather would utter
Anytime something broke down
Or cattle got out, and never once did
I think about what it meant. It was
Something to say to say something
Was off with the world. If it hadn't been
For us boys being there they might have
Said *motherfucker* instead. They didn't
Mean anything by it. Its meaning
Had faded after years of thoughtless use
Like the meaning of the word *hallelujah*.
This was why they reached for it throughout
The day the way they reached
For their pocketknives,
Soft, oft-handled things
In which a blade was folded.

ATOMIC FIREBALL

The quiet boy in the back of the bus
Has been handed something
He doesn't understand.
The bully who gave it to him
Has never once been kind to him,
And so this gift, this smooth red ball,
Is more than just a piece of candy.
It's an apology for every time
The bully whispered, "You stink,"
Every time he pinched his nose
And said, "Oink, oink, oink,"
Every time he called him "Miss Piggy"
In the presence of Laura Bauman.
No longer is it the quiet boy's fault
His father is a hog farmer.
"What are you waiting for?"
The bully says. "If you don't want it
I'll give it to somebody else."
The others rest their chins
On the seatbacks to watch
The boy put it in his mouth.
He wants to spit it out but knows
He can't, switches it from cheek
To cheek until his eyes water.
Under their laughter
He hears the bully say,
"Now you know how we feel
When you raise your hand."

SOAP OPERAS

Those summer days the sun would raise
The smell of warm carpet and Pine-Sol
Dust mites drifting like plankton
Through the baleen of the sunbeams
She would put soap operas on for company
While she cleaned I remember
Their peculiar muteness
Like when your ears won't pop
After the descent
So caught up were the characters
In their dramas they didn't notice
Me watching them
Sometimes she'd take a yellow cloth
Soft as baby clothes
And wipe the static and dust
Off the screen
But their expressions didn't change
For all her waving
Their voices rising in argument
As they paced a living room I never saw
Anyone dusting but which was always so clean

THE BLIND

The hunters who obtained permission
From our father to fire at the flocks
That passed southward over our land
Every autumn concealed themselves
Behind a blind of chicken wire stuffed
With cornhusks. Thermoses twisted
Tight on columns of black coffee,
They watched the gray sky for geese
While we watched the hunters from the burn pile
We were forbidden from passing beyond,
As if we were the ones in danger.
To draw the living down to where
The guns might touch them, they set
A flock of decoys to grazing in the field.
Each had a long spike for driving it
Into the ground. On their bellies,
Gold stickers that read: *Made in China*.
When the hunters went home we walked
Amongst them, frozen in whatever poses
They'd been fashioned in, doomed to hunger
Forever for the corn the combine had missed.
Their eyes were red beads. Blind, their purpose
Was to be seen, to reassure the living that
Their kind had deemed our farm a refuge,
Where spilled corn was abundant
And they would come to no harm.

THE BOMBING OF HOSPITALS

There was a time when they were kept far
Away from the front. Unafraid for their lives,
The nurses moved calmly through the wards
Carrying trays of shrapnel stewed in blood.
Days were slow. Letters came to say that,
Elsewhere, babies were being born, novels
Being published, plays being produced.
The letters, which had already been opened
By the time they reached the men they were
Addressed to, said, between the lines, that
There was a world yet untouched by the war,
A world they would be returning to once
They healed. Some of the letters contained
News from the front, far enough away to have
To be borne in the form of language,
Not as light and noise, and as the news
Of the latest battle was read out loud,
The war seemed like a nightmare they had
Had in common, and had woken from
Together, all at once.

There was time for flirtations to flare between
Nurses and patients, a few affairs. Smoking
Between amputations, the surgeons laughed
Under the trees, their bloody shirtsleeves
Rolled up, while in the garden convalescents
Hobbled about on crutches, played croquet,
Fell asleep in wheelchairs, apple blossoms

Fallen into their hair. Their only fear was that
Gangrene would set in, that they would be
The next to turn quiet and toward the wall.
They feared flies and bedsores, bad news
From home, the sudden appearance of a friend
Who'd been gravely wounded. But the hospital
Itself, built of bricks or boards, or composed
Of rows of linen tents pitched in a field
In a rush, was understood by all to be protected
By the presence of the wounded themselves,
Who knew no new harm could come to them,
Only the old harm find a firmer hold
And pull them under.

WOUNDED MEN SELDOM
COME HOME TO DIE

And this is why: when a wounded man comes home
To die he must come in through the summer kitchen,
Clutching his wound like a bunch of kindling.
At the sight of him his mother faints. He catches her

Just in time and lays her down on the floor.
When his sister comes in from slopping hogs to find her
Brother at the table with his long legs kicked out
And their mother senseless on the linoleum, she sighs

And unbuttons his shirt. The wound isn't visible yet,
It's still drifting around inside his body, bouncing
Under his skin like a man swimming under ice,
Desperate to find the place where he fell through.

When the wound surfaces, that's when she'll know
Whether he'll live or die. For now, his eyes are calm
And blue. He asks her which boys have been bothering her
At school. She knows not to ask him where he's been.

When their mother comes to, she insists she's fine.
"It's just this heat is all," she says. After putting a pot
Of coffee on, she says, "Now if you'll excuse me,
I'm going upstairs and close my eyes awhile."

There's blood soaking through his white tee shirt now.
His sister pretends not to see it. They talk through the evening.

Around midnight she tells him the sheets on his bed are clean.
He thanks her and tells her he might sit on the porch,

Watch fireflies like he used to when he was little.
In the morning his bed hasn't been slept in. There's no note
On the kitchen table, just a few fireflies in a Mason jar,
Holes punched in the tin lid so they can breathe.

ELEGY FOR THOMAS MERTON

*Do not think yourself better because you burn up friends and enemies
with long-range missiles without ever seeing what you have done.*
    —THOMAS MERTON, "Chant to Be Used in
    Processions around a Site with Furnaces"

The fan was manufactured for you.
Even as it blew on the bodies of innumerable
Sleepers it was dreaming of you.
All night it hawked its noise
Into the ears of others but yours was the name
It chanted. It was as if it was hunting you,
Though it never took a single step.

Instead, in the quiet Kentucky night your death
Came to the door, a letter the cold
And color of snow. Crossing the sea,
Folded over itself in the hold, it had obsessed
Over what it had to say to you, over your name
Scrawled languidly in a monk's quiet hand.
It knocked with its fist of pulp and postage

On the heavy oaken doors of the Abbey,
Waking the Brother in the guardhouse
Out of sitting sleep, who thought nothing
Of it when an envelope floated in. And when
You opened it at dawn, your fingers

Still swollen and dinged from woodcutting,
And saw your name scrawled there,

How could you not have answered its call?
Your last night at Gethsemani you lay
Awake in your hermitage, grinning
Like your Brothers in the grass. Your robes
Swept their graves as you passed
On your way into the dark chapel,
To bring yourself one last time before the icons'

Familiar flaws, the nick in Our Lady's forehead,
The patch of plaster missing from Christ's side.
Did you really believe you would ever kneel
In that pew again? Or, serving Mass
To your friends at the hermitage, whispering
Their first names as you offered them bread
And wine, did you know your death

Was a thin man with a face of blades
Standing in a bathroom in Thailand?
While you bathed he fanned you,
Clothed in voltage woven by turbines
Miles up river, where maybe a girl
Was even then picking her steps carefully
Along the bank, carrying a basket of laundry

Above the painless dismemberment
Of the waters. When you took hold
Of the fan's spine your every atom
Flashed impossibly bright, then dimmed.
The first man who tried to touch you
Was shocked an inch from your flesh.
They had to let your numinous power

Ebb out into the childish bathwater.
Someone called the State Department
("Good, now we don't have to shoot him.").
And you, who had written of the roar
Of bombers flying over your hermitage,
Your body was borne home with the bodies
Of the latest wave to die in the war.

PREMATURE ELEGY FOR
CLAUDE EATHERLY

Climbing the steps to the room you've taken
In New Orleans to kill yourself, you're aware
Of your shadow climbing beside you. How you wish
It would unhook itself from your body and remain,
A stain on the Victorian wallpaper, but it insists
On climbing with you, like a friend you wish
Would just let you go home alone when you're drunk.
In your pocket, a bottle, the pills kept chalk-dry
By cotton balls that remind you of the clouds that day.
You open the door, enter the room, see that you left
The window open. The curtains are swollen
With wind. You lie down on the bed and remember
Radioing Tibbets to tell him the weather was clear.
That was all you did. Stated that fact the way
A farmwife would. But you knew what it meant
To say that, and now you think you know
What it means to twist the cap off that bottle
And throw thirty white pills down the hatch.

WE DEFY AUGURY

Reading the word *inauguration* for the hundredth time
I caught it carrying the word *augur* inside it.
Augur, as in the priest in ancient Rome who was asked
To interpret the behavior of birds as a sign
Of divine approval or disapproval of some action
Being considered by the state. I see him on a hillside
Of olive trees, straining to hear whether they were
Calling in the branches where they had gathered
Or were silent. And if they took wing, squinting
To count their number and determine what sort
Of birds they were. Then observing which direction
They were flying. Whatever the answers, we know now
The birds were only looking to their own survival,
Obeying their hunger and their desire to mate,
Migrating if they sensed the seasons were turning
Against them. We know too that the augur was
Interpreting the birds' behavior based upon what
He thought the emperor wanted to do in his heart
Of hearts, or because he'd been bribed to say that
What the birds were doing meant this or that.
We know now it was all a sham. The words the favored
Daughter whispered in her father's ear where he sat
On his throne were the very words he'd told her
He would like to hear, words that boded well for her,
And for the birds who every autumn settled
In that olive orchard and were spared,
And for the augur walking back through the dark
Towards the glittering city, under his lucky stars.

THE MAN WITHOUT OXEN TREMBLES

*Take good note when you first hear the cranes flying over, coming each
year without fail and crying high in the heavens. They will give you
the sign for ploughing and tell when the winter's rains are at hand: at
their call the man without oxen trembles. Then give your oxen plenty
of fodder—if you have oxen. It is easy to say: "Please lend me your oxen
and wagon," easy also to answer, "I'm sorry, I've work for my own oxen."*
      —HESIOD, *Works and Days*

Last fall it was your neighbor
Who trembled when he heard their call.

Knowing he would ask to borrow your oxen
Upon seeing you walking in the wake

Of your last furrow, you opened more ground
Than you had seed to sow, driving your team

To exhaustion. This year you're the man
Without oxen. It is you who trembles

When the cranes fly over, crying down
To you that it's time to plough.

The harness you might have taken hold of
Last fall to still this shaking in your hands

Hangs on the barn wall, smelling faintly of lather.
Being a farmer, you know you didn't sow them

Deep enough, and that it won't be long now until
Winter rains bring their bones out of the hill.

SWATTING FLIES

You think of yourself now as having been
A sweet boy, the kind of kid
Who wouldn't hurt a fly,
But let us not forget that
In summer you kept a swatter nearby.

You liked the feel of the wire
Handle in your hand,
How easy it was
To wield, light and nimble
As a riding crop.

The business end was a square
Of blue plastic mesh, stippled
To let the air pass through
So that in the act of wrath
You didn't fan the fly to safety.

Granted, most days the killing
You did was passive. Sometimes
You even swatted your own bare calf,
Leaving a red welt
You felt vanish

Like the ring of condensation
Evaporating off the armrest
Of the chair in which you sat reading

Lord of the Flies.
But don't you remember

Those afternoons something
That had nothing to do with the flies
Incited you to slaughter them?
Then you had no sympathy for the ones
Who wrung their hands among

The breadcrumbs in the kitchen,
Begging you for mercy,
Or the ones you found
Making love on the windowsills
In the upstairs bedrooms

Where they had believed
Themselves safe.
The only thing that stopped you
Killing them was when
The blue square grew

So clogged with the dead
The living felt a breath of air
That made them take flight
Like people who flee a house
Moments before the drone strike.

THAT PARTICULAR VILLAGE

On October 22nd and 23rd, 2002, U.S. warplanes strafed the Afghan farming village of Chowkar-Karez, twenty-five miles north of Kandahar, killing at least ninety-three civilians. When asked about the incident at Chowkar, Secretary of Defense Donald Rumsfeld replied, "I cannot deal with that particular village."

Look, here's the thing. I can deal with that
Particular village about as well today
As I could deal with it yesterday, which is
To say, I cannot deal with that particular
Village at all. Other villages I can deal with,
Have dealt with and will deal with in the future,
But not that particular village. Look, think
Of the situation I'm in like this: I'm a tightrope
Walker in a circus tent in a prairie town in 1911.
I perform with my wife and without a net.
Unbeknownst to me my wife, who happens
To be a very beautiful woman, has fallen
In love with the tiger tamer. On this night,
While walking the tightrope towards her
Where she stands on the platform, I see
She has a big pair of golden garden shears
And she's preparing to cut the rope. Tell me,
What do I do? If I start to scream,
She'll cut the rope. If I say nothing,
She'll cut the rope. I can't deal with that
Village in particular because I really
Have to try and focus on sinking this

Putt. I can't deal with it today because
Tomorrow I'm flying to Chicago to participate
In the Associated Writing Programs Conference.
I've been invited to appear on a panel called
"Tangled Umbilical: What We Can Learn
From Paying Attention to Syntax in Political
Discourse and How We Can Use It to Write Better
Flash Fiction." I can't deal with that particular
Village because I was born in 1932. I cannot
Deal with it today or yesterday because
My senior thesis at Princeton was entitled
"The Steel Seizure Case of 1952 and Its Effect
On Presidential Powers." I can't deal with it
Because I have three children and six grand
Children none of whom will have to go
To the holy wars. I can't deal with that village,
That particular village, right now because I live
In Mount Misery, the former plantation
House where a young Frederick Douglass
Was sent to have his teen spirit broken
By the brutal slaveholder Edward Covey.
I can't because one day, after being beaten
Many times by his master, Douglass fought
Off Covey's cousin and then Covey himself
In the very yard where my wife grows camellias.
I can't because Douglass was never assaulted
By Covey again. I can't deal with that particular
Village in this life nor shall I be made to answer for
What happened there in the next. Certain things
About my past make it impossible for me
To deal with it: when I was little I was an Eagle
Scout, I wrestled in high school, I didn't graduate
From Georgetown Law. Nixon called me
A ruthless little bastard. I sold the company
I was CEO of to Monsanto for $12 million.

I cannot deal with that particular village.
I can't deal with it because once upon a time
I delivered a few pistols, some medieval
Spiked hammers, and a pair of golden cowboy
Boots to Saddam Hussein on behalf of
President Reagan. I can't deal with it because
A few years ago I had to make a special trip
To Abu Ghraib to personally turn up the volume
Of the Brandenburg Concertos to make a man's ears
Bleed more profusely. I can't deal because
On the afternoon of September 11th an aide
Scribbled down in shorthand what I was
Saying on the phone: "Best info fast—
Judge whether good enough hit Saddam
At same time—not only Bin Laden—
Need to move swiftly—Near term target
Needs—go massive—sweep it all up
—Things related and not." I can't . . . Look . . .
That particular village? That particular one.

DRONE

Defined as:

To make a sustained deep
Murmuring, humming, or buzzing
Sound; to talk in a persistently dull
Or monotonous tone; to live
In idleness like a drone
Bee (the male of the honeybee
That develops from an unfertilized egg,
Is larger and stouter than the worker,
Lacks a sting, takes no part in honey-gathering
Or care of the hive, is of use
To the colony only if a virgin queen
Requires insemination); to pass or proceed
In a dull, drowsy, or uneventful manner;
To utter or pronounce with a drone;
To pass or spend in idleness or in dull
Or monotonous activity; an unmanned
Aircraft or ship that is guided remotely.

Rhymes with:

Zone,
Phone,
Hone,
Shown,
Lone,
Flown,

Blown,
Stone,
Bone,
Moan,
Sewn,
Prone,
Condone,
Unknown,
Atone.

THE WITNESS TREE

One spring day two men turned up the lane
At the end of which the witness tree stood
To mark where what was no longer
One man's land ended and what was
No longer another man's began.

They wanted to know what the witness tree had seen,
But it refused to tell them
About the murders of crows,
The disorderly conduct of frogs in the pond,
The embezzlement of the moon by the Bank of Clouds
And its counterfeiting in a thousand waters.

Finally, the men threw up
Their hands and drove away.

Summer came and the men with it.
Again, they asked the witness tree
To tell them what it had seen.
Again it declined to say anything
About the shooting stars,
The misdemeanor of the mist,
The abduction of the field mice,
The barbwire-tapping of the pasture . . .

Losing patience, the men began planting
Flags at the corners of a square

The witness tree found itself standing
In the center of, as if under suspicion.

Then they drove away.

Autumn came and went.
Relieved, the witness tree let go
Of its green breath of leaves.
It stood naked and innocent,
Neither suspected of a crime
Nor questioned about something
It had seen.

But then, just when the sky was issuing
The first subpoenas of snow,
The men showed up again.

Hitched to the truck was a wood chipper.
In the bed were chainsaws and chaps,
Cans of gas and oil.

They gave the witness tree one last chance
To tell them what it had seen.
Afraid, the witness tree opened its mouth,
Prepared to describe how the hunter had killed the doe
Despite the white tail she'd raised in surrender,
How the moon had been laundering its light,
How the ice had forged the signatures of the branches
One night, and in the morning disappeared.

But no words escaped its lips.
Having vowed to keep the earth's secrets,
The witness tree stood silent.

The men sighed and began cutting.
They took turns, stopping often as if to give
The witness tree a chance to talk, though
It was becoming increasingly unreliable.
After it fell they bucked its body up into chunks
And fed its fingers and hands into the chipper
And tore its roots out by the hair
And ground its stump into dust.

Where the witness tree once stood
A witness house now stands.
It sees plenty
But no one thinks to question it.

III

CICADAS

We found their shells on the oldest oaks,
Backs blown open where they'd fled themselves.

There was always a moment before
We touched them when we'd loom near

Enough to stare into their amber chambers
As, once, in a hall of armor in the Art

Institute of Chicago, I stared through
The flanged hole the sword had bored.

But in the shells not a darkness but a light
Like that which I imagine seethes through

The keyholes of treasure chests
In sunken ships. No matter with what care

We picked them off, they always left behind
A leg or two like the crampons of climbers

Who've fallen. Sick now in this city
Far from where I like to imagine the ones

We never found are still clinging to the bark
Of the highest branches, I wish I could leave

My body blown open upon this bed
For a boy to find and carry

Up to a farmhouse, cupped gently
In his hand so as not to crush it.

FLYOVER COUNTRY

A storm hovers over my homeland,
The lobes of the thunderhead
Flaring with lightning the way
I imagine those of the brain
Flare with memory.
Looking down through
The window of the plane,
I fear for whoever lives
In that farmhouse now.
I remember,
Before rain, how the cows
Would lie down in the pasture
Like footsore pilgrims.
The sound a piece of tin
Nailed to the granary roof
Would make when the wind
Picked at it like a scab.
The way the leaves turned
White as if the maples were surrendering.
If it looked bad enough dad
Would call from the barn to tell us
To go down into the cellar,
Where jars of preserves put up
By the wives of the dead
Hired hands who'd lived
In that house before we did
Held all that remained
Of the kitchen gardens they tended

In the thirties, weird lanterns
Glowering with the threat
Of botulism. In the chest
Freezer, the cuts of the steer
We had slaughtered every year,
The butcher paper marked
Chuck, Rib, Loin, Shank
In black Sharpie. The spiders
In the insulation mistaking
The way the thunder made
Their webs tremble for prey.
And, in the corner,
That gentle thing that softened
Our hard water
For the sake of our mother's hair.

DARK DAY

Birds that had sung all morning
Fell quiet in the branches
Like the ampersands in a sentence
A boy doesn't know how to say.
Candles were lit midday
To read the Bible by.
A father asked his sons
To take turns reading prophecies
Their generation was blessed
To see come to pass.
They too believed
The end was near at hand.
Even the rebellious daughter
Who mouthed her prayers at supper
Felt afraid when she parted
Her bedroom curtains and saw stars.
But in the family plot their dead
Stayed dead. They'd expected
The clamor of coffin bells
Rung by ancestors resurrected,
But the tongues hung still.
When they heard
Their father snoring,
The boys stopped reading,
While upstairs their sister
Unbraided and brushed her hair.

It had become clear
To each of them separately,
The world wasn't ending,
Only growing darker.

WHITE LIE

Christmas Eves our dad would bring
Home from the farm real hay
For the reindeer that didn't exist
And after we were finally asleep
Would go out and take the slabs
Up in his arms and carry them
Back to the bed of his pickup,
Making sure to litter the snow
With chaff so he could show us
In the morning the place where
They'd stood eating, their harness
Bells dulled by the cold, their breath
Steam, all while we were dreaming.

THE CAPACITY OF SPEECH

It is easy to be decent to speechless things.
To hang houses for the purple martins
To nest in. To bed down the horses under
The great white wing of the year's first snow.
To ensure the dog and cat are comfortable.
To set out suet for the backyard birds.
To put the poorly shot, wounded deer down.
To nurse its orphaned fawn until its spots
Are gone. To sweep the spider into the glass
And tap it out into the grass. To blow out
The candle and save the moth from flame.
To trap the black bear and set it free.
To throw the thrashing brook trout back.
How easy it is to be decent
To things that lack the capacity of speech,
To feed and shelter whatever will never
Beg us or thank us or make us ashamed.

N JUDAH

After putting his earrings in
The man with the pinstriped pants
And the white lily starts crying

When we reach his stop
He can't carry everything
He has off the train

He has to come back
For the last grim-mouthed
Suitcase wiping his face

With the backs of his hands
His earrings dangling
Long and silver

No one rises to help him
He leaves
The lily on the seat

It makes us all turn
Quiet like a gift
You get

From an uncle you thought
Didn't love anyone
A few days after Christmas

BREAK IN THE WEATHER

Tiptoeing through the hieroglyphics
Scrawled pinkly on the walk
On your morning way to work
Is to you the worst thing about the rain
That has passed on in the night
Giving leave to the sun to come out
And roast them in these shapes
They've assumed and which always
Seem intentional like marks
Of punctuation in some lost lexicon
That would be meaningful to us
Had we the key to understand it
Some are laid out as if with a ruler
Others have spiraled inward as if
One end sought what the other knew
You know yourself to be yourself
By the way you look down and wince
And you know the people you are
Walking with are other people
By the way they stare straight ahead
Mashing this exquisite language
Into pink pulp but it isn't as simple
As that you tiptoers are benevolent
While the stare-straight-aheaders are cruel
Rather you are the metaphorical ones
For whom this carnage means more
Than it could possibly mean

To these brainless who
Sensing a change was coming
Fled their long homes
To solemnize the break in the weather

DEAD DOGS

Where are they now?
I would say that
Dead they are more alive
Than they were in life

When they were as close
As my shadow, as taken
For granted, loping a little
Behind me.

They became what
They longed for: bones.
I see them now,
Zia and Nova and Red.

Where did that moment go
When I knelt down and,
Shivering with a love
For what they were

Just a symbol of, embraced
Them wildly, their blood-
Flecked eyes rolling whitely
Over my shoulder

In the ecstasy of being
So suddenly regarded?

This poem seems proof
That that moment sank

Into me, leaving them
In the fast-fading afterglow
Of knowing themselves
Beloved of boys.

GROWING COLD

There was a time when I could be wounded
By something the moon did.

When the sight of my mother kneading dough
Sent me out into the snow.

When something my father said
Drove a green lance in my side.

When I had to put the book down
In awe of all the dead knew.

When it took me hours to prepare
To visit the ailing mare.

Now, I've built a castle and armed myself
With buckets of boiling tar and arrows.

Stocked the moat with fish with knives
For teeth. Cleared the trees for miles.

I can just see to where the far woods faint upwards,
Steep and green. In that bower cower

All those once-beloved things,
Come to do me harm.

How vigilant I am!
I don't even look up to watch the moon

Catapult over me nightly, though I know it
By my shadow.

LAMENT OF THE MAN WHO
PICKS UP DEAD ANIMALS

Give me the soil twelve dead horses
Displace and nothing else and I swear
I could live a good life and not worry
That my kids will be embarrassed to say
What it is their father does when asked

But give me those same twelve horses
Alive and breathing in their stalls
Waiting to be brushed and I will fail
Them miserably I will fail them
And they'll be forced to lie

COUNTRY THINGS

Some days even nature seems sinister.
Walking around the farm with a beer,
Seeking some solace after the evening news,
You meet the cat you love coming back
From the windbreak, a rare songbird
In his mouth. In the mulberry branches
The silkworms writhe in nests that, backlit
By twilight, look like X-rays of lungs.
In the pasture the cow kicks at her calf
And won't let her nurse, while in a seam
Of gleaming honey in the oak that lightning
Cleaved the queen daintily eats her offspring.
In the rafters of the barn the starlings are
Pushing the owls' eggs out of the nest,
While the owl herself is out hunting.
Going in, you nearly step on a swarm
Of ants ravishing a butterfly like pirates
Tearing a capsized ship down, its wings
Like torn sails, and the first thing you hear
When you enter the kitchen is the snap
Of the mousetrap you set this morning,
Tired of being kept awake all night
By their scratching in the walls. And so
You are met with your own small act
Of cruelty, your contribution to the whole.
With a pair of pliers that are themselves
Always biting something, you take
The broke-necked mouse by the tail

And throw it into the darkening yard,
Never knowing that in favor of it the cat
Let go of the bird, who was only stunned,
And whose song you woke to this morning.

ODE TO FLOUR

I was feeling down and wanted to praise
Something harmless, something we don't
Necessarily need, but that I'm glad
We have, and I lit just now upon flour.

I suppose flour could be harmful if
You don't eat wheat, but let's assume
You do. Think: where did your mother
Keep the flour when you were a child,

Or your father? Perhaps it was your father
Who did the baking. Maybe neither
Your mother nor your father baked
But they still kept some flour around,

Leftover from Christmas, or because
A neighbor had brought some over,
Though why a neighbor would bring
Flour over and then leave without it,

I don't know. Anyway you can tell
I want there to have been flour
In your childhood kitchen, in a paper bag
That gave off a little gasp of powder

Every time it was opened, which wasn't often.
On the side of the bag, a girl in a dress

Tiptoed amongst hens, a wicker basket
On her arm, and it was understood

She was bringing bread to the sick
And poor. Or maybe your family stored
The flour in a glass jar with a wire lid
That latched, or in a stoneware canister

With the word *Flour* painted in blue
Cursive on the side. Wherever it was,
Maybe you reached your hand inside
Every now and then to wonder

At how something so dry could feel
So cool that it felt damp. Or maybe
This is the wrong poem for you.
Maybe you loved salt.

THINGS WE DON'T OFTEN THINK OF

The gentleness
    of beekeepers.
The deer
    with one antler.
The fathers
    of murderers.
The birth
    pangs of cats.
The dreams
    of the mail carrier.
The deaf
    watching lightning.
The obituaries
    of distant towns.
The taxi driver
    driving home.
The barber
    sweeping up hair.
The basement
    in the house in the painting.
The backs
    of hand mirrors.
The hands
    that grew this food.
The hands
    that sewed this shirt.
The pens
    of old love letters.

The fossils
        in gravel quarries.
The ferns
        in the gas tank.
The music
        boxes in sunken ships.
The darkness
        in the accordion.
The night-reading
        of fishermen.
The skeletons
        of astronauts.
The grave
        of the undertaker.
The other side
        of the coffin pillow.

FILM OF THE BUILDING OF A
COFFIN VIEWED IN REVERSE

The little tacks that pinned the satin in fall out
Like baby teeth. The satin passes back through
Its fantasy of becoming a prom dress: it returns
Totally to the silkworms in the mulberry.
The pillow blows apart and the down darts
Back into the plucked goose. The black lab
Swims backwards with the bird in his mouth:
The goose flutters up into the sky and flies
Backwards with the flock into the north country
As the shell inhales the lead shot and the shell
Itself returns to the oiled dark of the gun.
The hammer kisses the nails back out of the wood.
The nails pass from his white lips to his dark pockets.
The screws spin out on the roads of brass
And the boards part ways. The boards, of heavy
Ash, lay stacked along the wall for a night.
The hands of the clock over the workbench
Spin wildly counterclockwise. Come morning
The boards return to the mill and converge
Into trees that float back into the woods
In search of their stumps like the phantom
Limbs of amputees. They know which ones
Are theirs by the rings, swing up onto them
And heal. The birds that were scared off
By the roar of the chainsaw come back. The dead

Man gets up off the floor and his broken cup
Becomes whole again. He puts it to his lips
And fills it with coffee from his mouth,
Coffee that grows hotter and blacker.

THE TWAIN

The one who has walked for years
Alongside you may one day

Fall behind you. One moment
They are there and the next

They are nowhere
In sight. In vain you turn

To see where it is
They have gone, and it is then

You notice this
Road you have been on

For so long and always
Thought was straight

Bends, so that if you were to
Walk for a thousand years

You might come full circle
To the place you set out from

With the one who was always
Beside you until they weren't.

This happened long ago.
You are still standing on that road,

Waiting. You have been waiting
For so long you have forgotten

Which of the twain you are:
The one who kept walking or

The one who fell behind.

FEATHERS

I want to be alone,
      not forever
But for a while, alone
      as some feathers
In the bed of a pickup,
      white ones
Plucked by the hands
      of a boy
Made shy by
      the kindness
Of his father.

I want to be forgotten
      that way, to drift
Up out of the bed
      and fall all over
The back roads named
      after dead farmers,
To settle light as dry
      flies on black
Water, to be mistaken
      for something
Commonplace, to deceive,
      so that when
The moon comes
      up, the dead
Roads go flying.

THE LIGHT AT THE END

The light at the end of the lane
The light at the end
Fashioned from late sun passing through green leaves
And the glow of fresh gravel not three days from the quarry
Down this lane let's set you walking
Towards the light at the end of the lane
The light at the end
And let's run a creek through a corrugated pipe
Sunk in the gravel so you have something to cross over
To mark how far you are yet
From the light at the end of the lane
The light at the end
And alongside you let's walk an old dog
With burrs and ticks in his fur
Not to protect you from anything
For if you're walking this lane you're beyond harm
But for companionship as you make your way
Towards the light at the end of the lane
The light at the end
Several birds have volunteered to stay on longer
To sing for you as you walk
Towards the light at the end of the lane
The light at the end
We hear you like beer so we hereby slip a bottle
Of something good and cold in your hand
To keep you refreshed as you approach
The light at the end of the lane
The light at the end

And to put things in perspective so that you may
Know you are still on Earth as you walk
Towards the light at the end of the lane
The light at the end
We'll hang a crescent moon on the eastern sky
Something to know where you are by
It's just dark enough now
To set flickering fireflies in the fields
That stretch away on either side
But remember the light in their abdomens
Is different from the light at the end of the lane
The light at the end
We don't know what else we can offer you as you walk
What more could you ask for
Save maybe that the lane grow longer
And the light linger
The light dwindling at the end of the lane
The light fading at the end

Notes

Jason Molina, "Heart My Heart": The lyrics in the epigraph are reprinted with permission, copyright ©2012 *Autumn Bird Songs*, all rights administered by Secretly Canadian Publishing.

"To Go to Lena": This poem was inspired by Adam Zagajewski's poem "To Go to Lvov."

"American Glue Factory": I learned about Rachel Carson's childhood, and her family's proximity to the American Glue Factory, from "How 'Silent Spring' Ignited the Environmental Movement," an essay by Eliza Griswold, published in *The New York Times Magazine* (September 21, 2012).

"Wounded Men Seldom Come Home to Die": The title is taken from Stephen Crane's collection of poems, *The Black Riders and Other Lines*.

"Elegy for Thomas Merton": The quote that prefaces this poem is from Thomas Merton's poem, "Chant to Be Used in Processions around a Site with Furnaces." From *The Collected Poems of Thomas Merton*, copyright ©1963 by The Abbey of Gethsemani, Inc., 1977 by The Trustees of the Merton Legacy Trust. Reprinted by permission of New Directions Publishing Corp.

"We Defy Augury": The phrase is from *Hamlet* (Act 5, Scene 2). "HAMLET: We defy augury. There's a special providence in the fall of a sparrow. If it be now, 'tis not to come. If it be not to come, it will be now. If it be not now, yet it will come—the readiness is all."

"Premature Elegy for Claude Eatherly": Claude Eatherly was piloting a plane called Straight Flush above Hiroshima on August 6, 1945. By reporting that the weather was clear, he effectively gave the signal for the Enola Gay to drop the atomic bomb. His suicide attempt was unsuccessful.

"The Man without Oxen Trembles": The title, and the quote that follows, are taken from Hesiod's *Works and Days*, translated by Hermann Fränkel.

"That Particular Village": The strafing of Chowkar-Karez, and Rumsfeld's response to questions regarding the incident, are described in *Dying Empire: U.S. Imperialism and Global Resistance* by Francis Shor. Rumsfeld's words at the end of the poem, from "Best info fast . . ." to ". . . things related and not," are actual orders Rumsfeld issued on September 11, 2001, jotted down by Stephen Cambone, a senior policy official in the administration (*The History of American Foreign Policy: From 1895* by Jerald A. Combs).

"Drone": The various definitions of the word are drawn from the *Merriam-Webster Dictionary*.

Acknowledgments

Many thanks to the editors of the journals in which the following poems first appeared, sometimes in different forms:

Modern Haiku: "Toy soldier . . ." and "One cork pushed in . . ."

New England Review: "Growing Cold" and "Film of the Building of a Coffin Viewed in Reverse"

POETRY Magazine: "Factory Town"

Prairie Schooner: "Apparition of Knives"

RATTLE: "We Defy Augury"

Spoon River Poetry Review: "To Go to Lena" and "The Vampire"

The New Yorker: "Chekhov"

The Threepenny Review: "Street Performer: Asheville, North Carolina" and "The Capacity of Speech"

ZYZZYVA: "Building a Temple for the Field Mice"

The poem "That Particular Village" appeared in the Library of America anthology, *War No More: Three Centuries of American Antiwar and Peace Writing.*

Thank you to the Aninstantia Foundation for a grant that supported the completion of this collection, and the members of Poets' Table for your friendship.

Thank you to everyone at Princeton University Press, especially Susan Stewart, Ellen Foos, Anne Savarese, Thalia Leaf, Jodi Price, and Jodi Beder.

Finally, thank you to Holly Mulder-Wollan for understanding why I have to touch down in "flyover country" every now and again.

Princeton Series of Contemporary Poets

Almanac: Poems, Austin Smith

An Alternative to Speech, David Lehman

And, Debora Greger

An Apology for Loving the Old Hymns, Jordan Smith

Armenian Papers: Poems l954–l984, Harry Mathews

At Lake Scugog: Poems, Troy Jollimore

Before Recollection, Ann Lauterbach

Blessing, Christopher J. Corkery

Boleros, Jay Wright

Carnations: Poems, Anthony Carelli

The Double Witness: Poems, 1970–1976, Ben Belitt

A Drink at the Mirage, Michael J. Rosen

Erosion, Jorie Graham

The Eternal City: Poems, Kathleen Graber

The Expectations of Light, Pattiann Rogers

An Explanation of America, Robert Pinsky

First Nights: Poems, Niall Campbell

Flyover Country: Poems, Austin Smith

For Louis Pasteur, Edgar Bowers

A Glossary of Chickens: Poems, Gary J. Whitehead

Grace Period, Gary Miranda

Hybrids of Plants and of Ghosts, Jorie Graham

In the Absence of Horses, Vicki Hearne

The Late Wisconsin Spring, John Koethe

Listeners at the Breathing Place, Gary Miranda

Movable Islands: Poems, Debora Greger

The New World, Frederick Turner

Night Talk and Other Poems, Richard Pevear

The 1002nd Night, Debora Greger

Operation Memory, David Lehman

Pass It On, Rachel Hadas

Poems, Alvin Feinman

The Power to Change Geography, Diana O'Hehir

Radioactive Starlings: Poems, Myronn Hardy

Reservations: Poems, James Richardson

Returning Your Call: Poems, Leonard Nathan

River Writing: An Eno Journal, James Applewhite

The Ruined Elegance: Poems, Fiona Sze-Lorrain

Sadness and Happiness: Poems, Robert Pinsky

Scaffolding: Poems, Elena Rivera

Selected Poems, Jay Wright

Shores and Headlands, Emily Grosholz

Signs and Wonders: Poems, Carl Dennis

Stet: Poems, Dora Malech

Syllabus of Errors: Poems, Troy Jollimore

The Tradition, Albert F. Moritz

The Unstill Ones: Poems, Miller Oberman

The Two Yvonnes: Poems, Jessica Greenbaum

Visiting Rites, Phyllis Janowitz

Walking Four Ways in the Wind, John Allman

Wall to Wall Speaks, David Mus

A Wandering Island, Karl Kirchwey

The Way Down, John Burt

Whinny Moor Crossing, Judith Moffett

A Woman Under the Surface: Poems and Prose Poems, Alicia Ostriker

Yellow Stars and Ice, Susan Stewart